FAVORITE
CHRISTMAS
CAROLS

FAVORITE
CHRISTMAS
CAROLS

with arrangements by Sarah Shaw

Carroll & Graf Publishers, Inc.
New York

Published under license from Michael O'Mara Books, Ltd., London (England)
First Carroll & Graf edition 1997

Carroll & Graf Publishers, Inc.
19 W. 21st Street
New York, NY 10010

ISBN: 0-7867-0459-4

Manufactured in the United States of America

Contents

CHRISTMAS is a time for celebrating
and what better way to get you in the Christmas mood than
singing and playing favourite carols.
Although the tradition of singing carols at Christmas
goes back over five hundred years, this book remembers
the Victorian Age, when many Christmas 'traditions',
such as Christmas cards and Christmas trees,
were invented. Above all, children would gather round
the piano with their parents to sing Christmas
songs and carols.

Now you too can sing and play your favourite carols to
the traditional tunes. Easy-to-play music arrangements
for the piano accompany a complete set of verses of
each carol — and there are also guitar-chord symbols so
the whole family can take part!

Whether you are huddled round the fire on Christmas Eve
or carol-singing in your neighbourhood, you will
soon find that this beautifully illustrated book of carols
will become a treasured part of your
Christmas celebrations.

AWAY IN A MANGER

TUNE: W J Kirkpatrick

Away in a manger, no crib for a bed,
The little Lord Jesus laid down His sweet head.
The stars in the bright sky looked down where He lay,
The little Lord Jesus asleep on the hay.

The cattle are lowing, the Baby awakes,
But little Lord Jesus no crying He makes.
I love Thee, Lord Jesus! Look down from the sky
And stay by my side until morning is nigh.

Be near me, Lord Jesus – I ask Thee to stay
Close by me for ever and love me, I pray.
Bless all the dear children in Thy tender care
And fit us for heaven to live with Thee there.

WORDS: Anon

THE FIRST NOEL

Tune: English Traditional

THE FIRST NOEL the angel did say
Was to certain poor shepherds in fields as they lay –
In fields where they lay keeping their sheep
On a cold winter's night that was so deep.

Noel, Noel, Noel, Noel,
Born is the King of Israel.

They looked up and saw a star
Shining in the East beyond them far,
And to the Earth it gave great light,
And so it continued both day and night.

Chorus

And by the light of that same star
Three wise men came from country far.
To seek for a king was their intent
And to follow the star wherever it went.

Chorus

This star drew nigh to the north-west.
O'er Bethlehem it took its rest,
And there it did both stop and stay
Right over the place where Jesus lay.

Chorus

Then entered in those wise men three
Full reverently upon their knee
And offered there, in His presence,
Their gold and myrrh and frankincense.

Chorus

Then let us all with one accord
Sing praises to our Heavenly Lord
That hath made Heaven and earth of nought,
And with His blood mankind hath bought.

Chorus

WORDS: ENGLISH TRADITIONAL

GOOD KING WENCESLAS

TUNE: FROM 'PIAE CANTIONES'

GOOD KING WENCESLAS look'd out
On the Feast of Stephen,
When the snow lay round about
Deep and crisp, and even.
Brightly shone the moon that night,
Though the frost was cruel,
When a poor man came in sight,
Gath'ring winter fuel.

King:	'Hither, page, come stand by me. If though know'st it telling, Yonder peasant, who is he, Where and what his dwelling?'
Page:	'Sire, he lives a good league hence Underneath the mountain, Close against the forest fence By Saint Agnes' fountain!'
King:	'Bring me flesh and bring me wine, Bring me pine logs hither. Thou and I, we'll see him dine, When we bear them thither.'
All:	Page and monarch forth they went, Forth they went together, Through the rude wind's wild lament And the bitter weather.

Page:	'Sire the night is darker now And the storm grows stronger. Fails my heart, I know not how, I can go no longer.'
King:	'Mark my footsteps, good my page, Tread thou in them boldly. Thou shalt find the winter's rage Freeze thy blood less coldly.'

All:	In his master's steps he trod, Where the snow lay dinted; Heat was in the very sod Which his foot had printed. Therefore, Christian men, be sure, Wealth or rank possessing, Ye who now will bless the poor Shall yourselves find blessing.

Words: J M Neale

HARK! THE HERALD ANGELS SING

TUNE: MENDELSSOHN

Hark! The herald angels sing
Glory to the new-born King.
Peace on earth and mercy mild,
God and sinners reconciled.
Joyful all ye nations rise,
Join the triumph of the skies —
With th'angelic host proclaim,
'Christ is born in Bethlehem.'
Hark! The herald angels sing
Glory to the new-born King.

Christ by highest heav'n adored,
Christ the everlasting Lord,
Late in time behold Him come
Offspring of a virgin's womb.
Veiled in flesh the Godhead see,
Hail th'incarnate Deity!
Pleased as man with man to dwell,
Jesus our Emmanuel.
Hark! The herald angels sing
Glory to the new-born King.

Hail the heav'n-born Prince of Peace!
Hail the Sun of Righteousness!
Light and life to all He brings,
Risen with healing in His wings.
Mild, He lays His glory by —
Born that man no more may die,
Born to raise the sons of earth,
Born to give them second birth.
Hark! The herald angels sing
Glory to the new-born King.

Words: C Wesley

O LITTLE TOWN OF BETHLEHEM

TUNE: ENGLISH TRADITIONAL

O LITTLE TOWN OF BETHLEHEM,
How still we see thee lie!
Above thy deep and dreamless sleep
The silent stars go by.
Yet in thy dark streets shineth
The everlasting light:
The hopes and fears of all the years
Are met in thee tonight.

O morning stars together
Proclaim the holy birth
And praises sing to God the King,
And peace to men on earth,
For Christ is born of Mary.
And gathered all above,
While mortals sleep, the angels keep
Their watch of wond'ring love.

How silently, how silently
The wondrous gift is given!
So God imparts to human hearts
The blessings of His heav'n.
No ear may hear his coming,
But in this world of sin,
Where meek souls will receive Him still,
The dear Christ enters in.

O holy Child of Bethlehem,
Descend to us, we pray;
Cast out our sin and enter in,
Be born in us today.
We hear the Christmas angels
The great glad tidings tell.
O come to us, abide with us,
Our Lord Emmanuel.

WORDS: P BROOKS

ONCE IN ROYAL DAVID'S CITY

TUNE: H J GAUNTLETT

Once in royal David's city
Stood a lowly cattle shed,
Where a mother laid her baby
In a manger for His bed.
Mary was that mother mild,
Jesus Christ her little child.

He came down to earth from heaven,
Who is God and Lord of all,
And His shelter was a stable,
And His cradle was a stall;
With the poor and mean and lowly,
Lived on earth our Saviour holy.

And through all His wondrous childhood
He would honour and obey,
Love and watch the lowly maiden
In whose gentle arms He lay.
Christian children all must be
Mild, obedient, good as He.

For He is our childhood's pattern,
Day by day like us He grew;
He was little, weak and helpless,
Tears and smiles like us He knew.
And He feeleth for our sadness,
And He shareth in our gladness.

And our eyes at last shall see Him,
Through His own redeeming love.
For that child so dear and gentle
Is our Lord in heaven above;
And He leads His children on
To the place where He is gone.

Not in that poor lowly stable,
With the oxen standing by,
We shall see Him, but in heaven,
Set at God's right hand on high;
When like stars His children crowned
All in white shall wait around.

WORDS: C F ALEXANDER

Christmas Greetings.

WHILE SHEPHERDS WATCHED

TUNE: 'ESTE'S PSALTER'

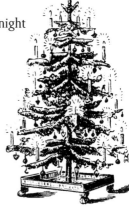

W HILE SHEPHERDS WATCHED their flocks by night
All seated on the ground,
The angel of the Lord came down
And glory shone around.

'Fear not,' said he (for mighty dread
Had seized their troubled mind).
'Glad tidings of great joy I bring
To you and all mankind.

'To you, in David's town, this day
Is born of David's line
A saviour who is Christ the Lord
And this shall be the sign:

'The heavenly Babe you there shall find
To human view displayed,
All meanly wrapped in swathing bands
And in a manger laid.'

Thus spake the Seraph, and forthwith
Appeared a shining throng
Of angels praising God, who thus
Addressed their joyful song:

'All glory be to God on high,
And to the earth be peace;
Goodwill henceforth from heaven to men
Begin and never cease!'

WORDS: NAHUM TATE

A Happy Christmas to You!

21

O COME, ALL YE FAITHFUL

TUNE: UNKNOWN

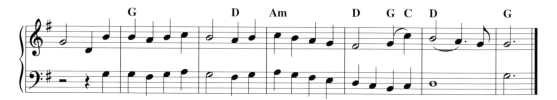

O COME, ALL YE FAITHFUL,
Joyful and triumphant,
O come ye, O come ye to
Bethlehem.
Come and behold him
Born the King of Angels:

O come, let us adore Him,
O come, let us adore Him,
O come, let us adore Him,
Christ the Lord!

God of God,
Light of Light,
Lo! he abhors not the Virgin's womb:
Very God,
Begotten, not created.

Chorus

See how the shepherds,
Summoned to His cradle,
Leaving their flocks, draw nigh with fear.
We too will thither
Bend our joyful footsteps.

Chorus

Sing, choirs of angels,
Sing in exultation.
Sing, all ye citizens of heav'n above:
Glory to God
In the highest.

Chorus

Yea, Lord, we greet Thee
Born this happy morning.
Jesu, to Thee be glory giv'n —
Word of the Father
Now in flesh appearing.

Chorus

WORDS: UNKNOWN

23

SILENT NIGHT

Tune: Franz Gruber

SILENT NIGHT, holy night,
All is calm, all is bright;
Round yon Virgin Mother and Child,
Holy Infant, so tender and mild;
Sleep in heavenly peace,
Sleep in heavenly peace.

Silent night, holy night,
Shepherds quake at the sight;
Glories stream from heaven afar,
Heavenly hosts sing alleluia;
Christ the Saviour is born,
Christ the Saviour is born.

Words: Josef Mohr

As with Gladness Men of Old

TUNE: C KOCHER

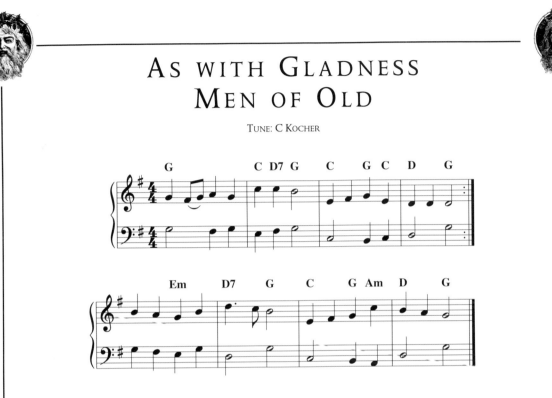

As with gladness men of old
Did the guiding star behold,
As with joy they hailed its light,
Leading onward, beaming bright,
So, most gracious Lord, may we
Ever more be led to Thee.

As with joyful steps they sped
To that lowly manger bed,
There to bend the knee before
Him whom heaven and earth adore,
So may we with willing feet
Ever seek thy mercy-seat.

As they offered gifts most rare
At Thy cradle rude and bare,
So may we with holy joy,
Pure and free from sin's alloy,
All our costliest treasures bring,
Christ, to Thee, our heavenly King.

Holy Jesus, every day
Keep us in the narrow way,
And, when earthly things are past,
Bring our ransomed souls at last
Where they need no star to guide,
Where no clouds Thy glory hide.

WORDS: W CHATTERTON DIX

ANGELS FROM THE REALMS OF GLORY

TUNE: FRENCH TRADITIONAL

Ａ NGELS FROM THE REALMS OF GLORY,
Wing your flight o'er all the earth.
Ye who sang creation's story,
Now proclaim Messiah's birth.

Come and worship,
Christ the new-born King,
Come and worship,
Worship Christ the new-born King.

Shepherds in the field abiding,
Watching o'er your flocks by night;
God with man is now residing,
Yonder shines the infant light.

Chorus

Sages, leave your contemplations –
Brighter visions beam afar.
Seek the great desire of nations,
Ye have seen His natal star.

Chorus

Saints before the altar bending,
Watching long in hope and fear.
Suddenly the Lord, descending,
In His temple shall appear.

Chorus

Though an infant now we view Him,
He shall fill His Father's throne.
Gather all the nations to Him,
Every knee shall then bow down.

Chorus

WORDS: FRENCH TRADITIONAL

GOD REST YOU MERRY, GENTLEMEN

TUNE: ENGLISH TRADITIONAL

G OD REST YOU MERRY, GENTLEMEN, let nothing you dismay.
Remember Christ, our Saviour, was born on Christmas Day
To save us all from Satan's power when we had gone astray,

O tidings of comfort and joy!
Comfort and joy,
O tidings of comfort and joy.

From God, our heavenly Father, a blessed angel came
And unto certain shepherds brought tidings of the same:
How that in Bethlehem was born The Son of God by name,

Chorus

The shepherds at those tidings rejoiced much in mind
And left their flocks a-feeding in tempest, storm and wind,
And went to Bethlehem straightway the Blessed Babe to find,

Chorus

But when to Bethlehem they came, whereat this infant lay,
They found Him in a manger, where oxen feed on hay.
His mother, Mary, kneeling, unto the Lord did pray,

Chorus

Now to the Lord sing praises, all you within this place,
And with true love and brotherhood each other now embrace.
This holy tide of Christmas as others doth deface,

Chorus

WORDS: ENGLISH TRADITIONAL

I Saw Three Ships

TUNE: ENGLISH TRADITIONAL

I SAW THREE SHIPS come sailing in
On Christmas Day, on Christmas Day.
I saw three ships come sailing in
On Christmas Day in the morning.

And what was in those ships all three
On Christmas Day, on Christmas Day?
And what was in those ships all three
On Christmas Day in the morning?

Our Saviour Christ and His lady
On Christmas Day, on Christmas Day.
Our Saviour Christ and His lady
On Christmas Day in the morning.

Pray, whither sailed those ships all three
On Christmas Day, on Christmas Day?
Pray whither sailed those ships all three
On Christmas Day in the morning?

O, they sailed in to Bethlehem
On Christmas Day, on Christmas Day.
O, they sailed in to Bethlehem
On Christmas Day in the morning.

And all the bells on earth shall ring
On Christmas Day, on Christmas Day.
And all the bells on earth shall ring
On Christmas Day in the morning.

And all the angels in heaven shall sing
On Christmas Day, on Christmas Day.
And all the angels in heaven shall sing
On Christmas Day in the morning.

And all the souls on earth shall sing
On Christmas Day, on Christmas Day.
And all the souls on earth shall sing
On Christmas Day in the morning.

Then let us all rejoice again
On Christmas Day, on Christmas Day.
Then let us all rejoice again
On Christmas Day in the morning.

WORDS: ENGLISH TRADITIONAL

IT CAME UPON THE MIDNIGHT CLEAR

TUNE: ENGLISH TRADITIONAL

IT CAME UPON THE MIDNIGHT CLEAR,
That glorious song of old,
From angels bending near the earth
To touch their harps of gold:
'Peace on earth, good will to men
From heaven's all-gracious King.'
The world in solemn stillness lay
To hear the angels sing.

Still through the cloven skies they come
With peaceful wings unfurled,
And still their heavenly music floats
O'er all the weary world.
Above its sad and lowly plains
They bend on hov'ring wing,
And ever o'er its Babel-sounds
The blessed angels sing.

Yet with the woes of sin and strife
The world has suffered long:
Beneath the angel-strain have rolled
Two thousand years of wrong,
And man, at war with man, hears not
The love-song which they bring.
O hush the noise, ye men of strife,
And hear the angels sing!

For lo! the days are hastening on
By prophet-bards foretold,
When, with the ever-circling years,
Comes round the age of gold:
When peace shall over all the earth
Its ancient splendours fling,
And the whole world send back the song
Which now the angels sing.

WORDS: E H SEARS

WE WISH YOU A MERRY CHRISTMAS

TUNE: WEST COUNTRY TRADITIONAL

WE WISH YOU A MERRY CHRISTMAS,
We wish you a merry Christmas,
We wish you a merry Christmas
And a happy New Year.

Good tidings we bring
To you and your kin.
We wish you a merry Christmas
And a happy New Year.

Now bring us some figgy pudding,
Now bring us some figgy pudding,
Now bring us some figgy pudding
And bring some out here.

Chorus

We all like figgy pudding,
We all like figgy pudding,
We all like figgy pudding,
So bring some out here.

Chorus

And we won't go until we've got some,
We won't go until we've got some,
We won't go until we've got some,
So bring some out here.

Chorus

WORDS: WEST COUNTRY TRADITIONAL

WE THREE KINGS
OF ORIENT ARE

TUNE: J H HOPKINS

WE THREE KINGS of ORIENT ARE
Bearing gifts we traverse afar —
Field and fountain, moor and mountain —
Following yonder star.

O star of wonder, star of night,
Star with royal beauty bright,
Westward leading, still proceeding,
Guide us to Thy perfect light.

Melchior: Born a King on Bethlehem's plain,
Gold I bring to crown Him again
King for ever, ceasing never,
Over us all to reign.

Chorus

Caspar: Frankincense to offer have I,
Incense owns a Deity nigh.
Prayer and praising, all men raising,
Worship him, God most High.

Chorus

Balthazar: Myrrh is mine – it's bitter perfume
Breathes a life of gathering gloom:
Sorrowing, sighing, bleeding, dying,
Sealed in a stone-cold tomb.

Chorus

Glorious now, behold Him arise:
King and God and sacrifice.
Heaven sings, 'Alleluia';
'Alleluia,' the earth replies.

Chorus

WORDS: J H HOPKINS

A mirthful, merry time this Christmas.

THE HOLLY AND THE IVY

TUNE: ENGLISH TRADITIONAL

THE HOLLY AND THE IVY,
When they are both full grown,
Of all the trees that are in the wood
The holly bears the crown.

The rising of the sun
And the running of the deer,
The playing of the merry organ,
Sweet singing in the choir.

The holly bears a blossom
As white as the lily flower,
And Mary bore sweet Jesus Christ
To be our sweet Saviour.

Chorus

The holly bears a berry
As red as any blood,
And Mary bore sweet Jesus Christ
To do poor sinners good.

Chorus

The holly bears a prickle
As sharp as any thorn,
And Mary bore sweet Jesus Christ
On Christmas Day in the morn.

Chorus

The holly bears a bark
As bitter as any gall,
And Mary bore sweet Jesus Christ
For to redeem us all.

Chorus

The holly and the ivy,
When they are both full grown,
Of all the trees that are in the wood
The holly bears the crown.

Chorus

WORDS: ENGLISH TRADITIONAL

GOOD CHRISTIAN MEN, REJOICE

TUNE: GERMAN TRADITIONAL

GOOD CHRISTIAN MEN, REJOICE
With heart and soul and voice.
Give ye heed to what we say:
News! News!
Jesus Christ is born today.
Ox and ass before him bow,
And he is in the manger now.
Christ is born today,
Christ is born today.

Good Christian men, rejoice
With heart and soul and voice.
Now ye hear of endless bliss:
Joy! Joy!
Jesus Christ was born for this.
He hath ope'd the heavenly door
And man is blessed evermore.
Christ was born for this,
Christ was born for this.

Good Christian men, rejoice
With heart and soul and voice.
Now ye need not fear the grave.
Peace! Peace!
Jesus Christ was born to save!
Calls you one and calls you all
To gain his everlasting hall:
Christ was born to save!
Christ was born to save!

WORDS: J M NEALE

SEE AMID THE WINTER'S SNOW

TUNE: JOHN GOSS

SEE AMID THE WINTER'S SNOW
Born for us on earth below.
See the tender Lamb appears,
Promised from eternal years.

Hail, thou ever blessed morn,
Hail, redemption's happy dawn.
Sing through all Jerusalem,
'Christ is born in Bethlehem.'

Lo! within a manger lies
He who built the starry skies.
He, who throned in heights sublime,
Sits amid the Cherubim.

Chorus

Say, ye holy shepherds, say
What your joyful news today?
Wherefore have ye left the sheep
On the lonely mountain steep?

Chorus

As we watched at dead of night,
Lo! we saw a wondrous light.
Angels singing peace on earth,
Told us of the Saviour's birth.

Chorus

Sacred Infant, all Divine,
What a tender love was Thine.
Thus to come from highest bliss,
Down to such a world as this.

Chorus

Teach, O teach us, Holy Child,
By thy face so meek and mild.
Teach us to resemble Thee
In Thy sweet humility.

Chorus

WORDS: E CASWALL

A merry CHRISTMAS

45

DING DONG! MERRILY ON HIGH

TUNE: FRENCH TRADITIONAL

DING DONG! MERRILY ON HIGH in heav'n the bells are ringing.
Ding dong! Verily the sky is riv'n with angel singing.
Gloria, Hosanna in excelsis!
Gloria, Hosanna in excelsis!

E'en so here below, below let steeple bells be swungen,
And i-o, i-o, i-o by priests and people sungen.
Gloria, Hosanna in excelsis!
Gloria, Hosanna in excelsis!

Pray you, dutifully prime your matin chime, ye ringers.
May you beautifully rime your evetime song, ye singers.
Gloria, Hosanna in excelsis!
Gloria, Hosanna in excelsis!

WORDS: G R WOODWARD